Who Lives in Trees?

Trish Holland

TeachingStrategies™ • Washington D.C.

For Teaching Strategies, Inc.
Publisher: Larry Bram
Editorial Director: Hilary Parrish Nelson
VP Curriculum and Assessment: Cate Heroman
Product Manager: Kai-leé Berke
Book Development Team: Sherrie Rudick and Jan Greenberg
Project Manager: Jo A. Wilson

For Q2AMedia
Editorial Director: Bonnie Dobkin
Editor and Curriculum Adviser: Suzanne Barchers
Program Manager: Gayatri Singh
Creative Director: Simmi Sikka
Project Manager: Santosh Vasudevan
Designer: Ritu Chopra
Picture Researcher: Stephanie Mills

Picture Credits
t-top b-bottom c-centre l-left r-right bg-baground

Cover: Nancy Kennedy/Dreamstime, Lezh/Istockphoto, Jens Stolt/Istockphoto.

Back Cover: David Whaley/Dreamstime.

Title page: Tom C Amon/Shutterstock.

Insides :Irin-k/Shutterstock: 3bg, CJMcKendry/Istockphoto: 3l, Maisan Caines/Dreamstime: 3r, Rene Drouyer/ Dreamstime: 4, Tom C Amon/Shutterstock: 5, Anthony Hathaway/Dreamstime: 6, Javarman/Shutterstock: 7bg, Satoshi Kuribayashi/Photolibrary: 7, Istockphoto: 8, Outdoorsman/Dreamstime: 9, Dan Kite/Istockphoto: 10, Nancy Kennedy/Dreamstime: 11, Paula Cobleigh/ Shutterstock: 12, Paula Cobleigh/Shutterstock: 12 CathyKeifer/Istockphoto: 13, Slawomir Kuter/Dreamstime: 14, Glen Gaffney/Dreamstime: 15, David Whaley/ Dreamstime: 16, Allen Sparks/Flickr: 17, asparks306/Flickr: 17 Craigrjd/Dreamstime: 18, Laure Niche/Istockphoto: 19, Timothy Craig Lubcke/Shutterstock: 20, PureStock/ Photolibrary: 21, Irochka/Dreamstime: 22t, René Mansi/ Irochka/Dreamstime:22+ Istockphoto: 22l, Sven Klaschik/ Istockphoto: 22r, Cedric Jacquet/Photolibrary:23+1 Shutterstock: 23t, Arnold John Labrentz/Shutterstock: 23bl, Keith Douglas/Photolibrary: 23br, Iakov Kalinin/ Shutterstock: 24.

Teaching Strategies, Inc.
P.O. Box 42243
Washington, DC 20015
www.TeachingStrategies.com

ISBN: 978-1-60617-131-8

Library of Congress Cataloging-in-Publication Data
Holland, Trish.
  Who lives in trees? / Trish Holland.
     p. cm.
  ISBN 978-1-60617-131-8
  1. Forest animals--Juvenile literature. I. Title.
  QL112.H65 2010
  591.73--dc22
                        2009044307

CPSIA tracking label information:
RR Donnelley, Shenzhen, China
Date of Production: February 2011
Cohort: Batch 2

Printed and bound in China

 2 3 4 5 6 7 8 9 10   15 14 13 12 11
        Printing   Year Printed

Whoo! Whoo!
Who lives in this tree?

With wings I can fly
to my nest way up high.
I am an **owl**.
I live in this tree.

Whoo! Whoo!
Who lives in this tree?

With strong tail and arms
I can swing all day long.
I am a **monkey**.
I live in this tree.

4

Whoo! Whoo!
Who lives in this tree?

With sticky little toes
I can cling upside down.
I am a **tree frog**.
I live in this tree.

Whoo! Whoo!
Who lives in this tree?

With long tail and claws
I can climb anytime.
I am an **anteater**.
I live in this tree.

Whoo! Whoo!
Who lives in this tree?

With skin stretched like wings
I can glide side to side.
I am a **flying dragon**.
I live in this tree.

Whoo! Whoo!
Who lives in this tree?

With wings I can fly
to my big buzzing hive.
I am a **bee**.
I live in this tree.

Whoo! Whoo!
Who lives in this tree?

I scrape out a den,
but it smells just a bit.
I am a **skunk**.
I live in this tree.

Whoo! Whoo!
Who lives in this tree?

With strong grip and claws
I hold on with my paws.
I am a **koala**.
I live in this tree.

Whoo! Whoo!
Who lives in this tree?

With wings I can flit
to a banquet on a branch.
I am a **ladybug**.
I live in this tree.

Whoo! Whoo!
Who lives in this tree?

With sharp, tiny claws
I can run just for fun.
I am a **squirrel**.
I live in this tree.

Whoo! Whoo!
Who lives in this tree?

With wings I can flutter
from my comfortable cocoon.
I am a **butterfly**.
I live in this tree.

Whoo! Whoo!
Who lives in this tree?

Hooks and claws on my feet
help me walk on my web.
I am a **spider**.
I live in this tree.

Whoo! Whoo!
Who lives in this tree?

With humming wings I dart
to the babies in my nest.
I am a **hummingbird**.
I live in this tree.

Whoo! Whoo!
Who lives in this tree?

With my muscles I can climb.
Then I make a cozy coil.
I am a **tree snake**.
I live in this tree.

Whoo! Whoo!
Who lives in this tree?

I fly to my nest.
My dead tree is the best.
I am a **woodpecker**.
I live in this tree.

Whoo! Whoo!
Who lives in this tree?

With wings I fly up.
Then I hang with head down.
I am a **bat**.
I live in this tree.

Whoo! Whoo!
Who lives in this tree?

With eggs in my nest
I sit warm in my nook.
I am a **bluebird**.
I live in this tree.

Whoo! Whoo!
Who lives in this tree?

With claws I dig tunnels.
Tree roots are my roof.
I am a **wombat**.
I live in this tree.

Whoo! Whoo!
Who lives in this tree?

No claws and no wings!
Our feet aren't sticky things.
We are just **kids**!
We play in this tree.

What is good for trees?

Sun

Soil

Rain